PLEASE BE KIND BY
SCANNING ME AND
GIVING A REVIEW

ABC

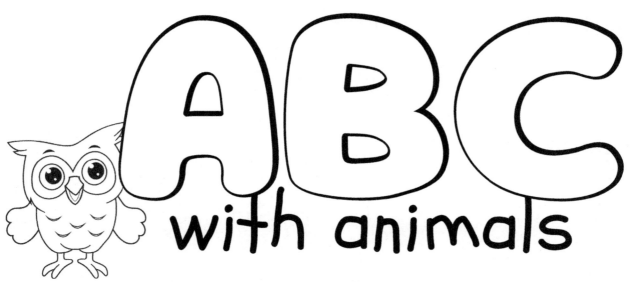

with animals

Learn the alphabet letters and numbers

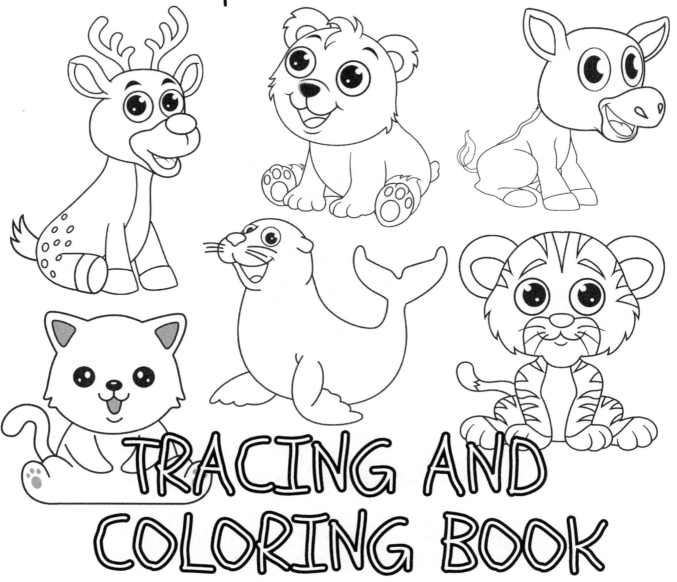

TRACING AND COLORING BOOK

This book belongs to:

_____

CONTENTS:

Part 1:

Trace straight and curved lines

Part 2:

Trace alphabet letters A – Z

Part 3:

Trace numbers 0 – 9

Bonus Part:

Trace sight words & Practice

Hallo!

Please give me some color...

Part 1

Trace straight and curved lines

It is essential for kids to learn pen control and refine pre-writing skills which gives the foundation for drawing and writing letters and words.

Develop hand-eye coordination and fine motor skills with these tracing exercises.

An adult's supervision (and sometimes assistance) is required throughout the use of this workbook.

Hallo!

Please give me some color....

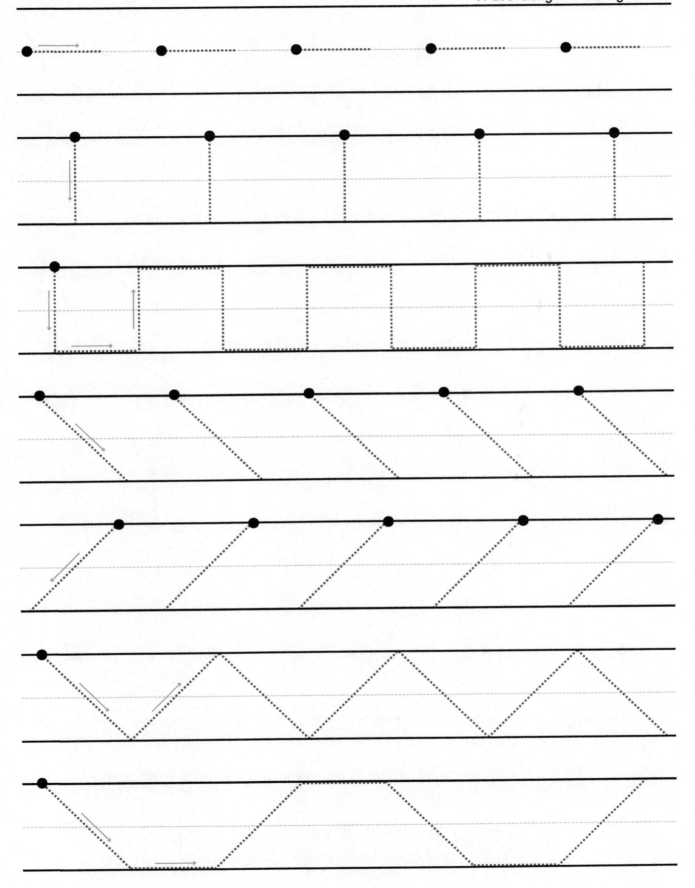

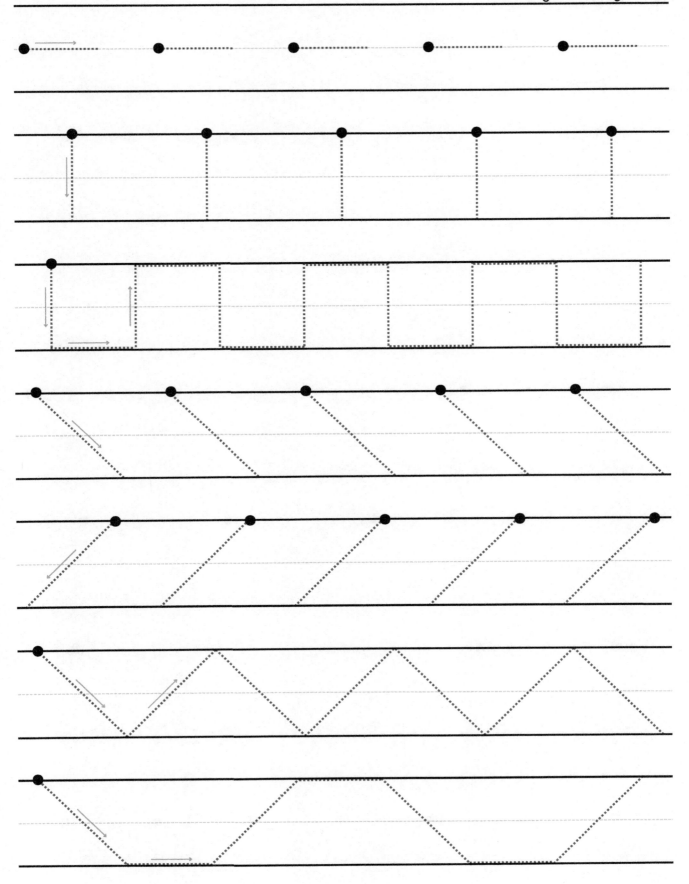

Part 2

Trace alphabet letters A – Z

Research has shown that tracing strengthens handwriting by helping children recognize the shape and letter while also practicing the appropriate size of the letter and correct formation of the letter.

Develop confidence to write the letters correctly by tracing the alphabet letters.

We can color in the pictures of each of the animals associated with the letter.

Hallo!

Please give me some color....

Aa

A is for Ape

Trace along the alphabet character

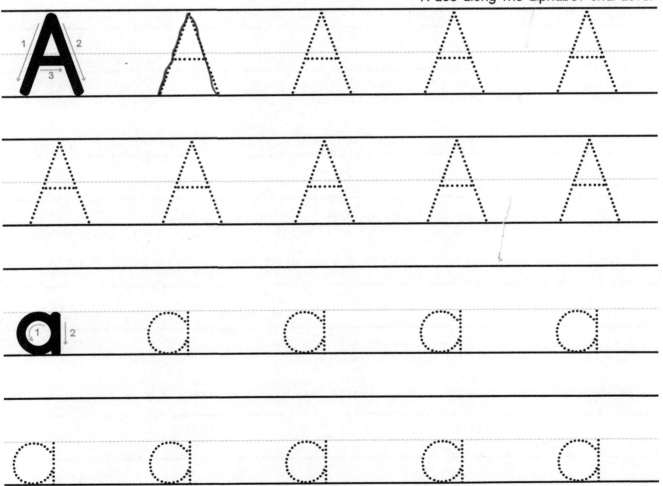

 # Let's start this journey!

Let's start this journey!

B b

B is for Bear

Trace along the alphabet character

B B B B B

B B B B B

b b b b b

b b b b b

We are on our way!

B B B B B

B B B B B

B B B B B

We are on our way!

b   b   b   b   b

b   b   b   b   b

b   b   b   b   b

b   b   b   b   b

C c

C is for Cat

Trace along the alphabet character

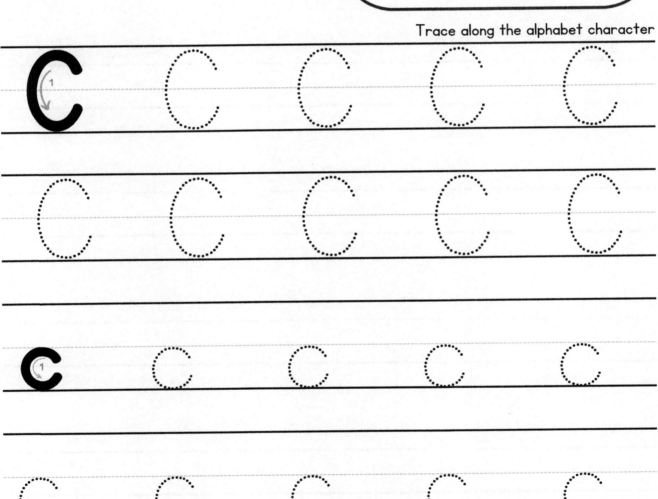

You are a cool cat!

a b c d e f g h i j k l m n o p q r s t u v w x y z

You are a cool cat!

c c c c c

c c c c c

c c c c c

Dd

D is for Dog

D D D D D

D D D D D

d d d d d

d d d d d

A B C (D) E F G H I J K L M N O P Q R S T U V W X Y Z

Let's be the top dog

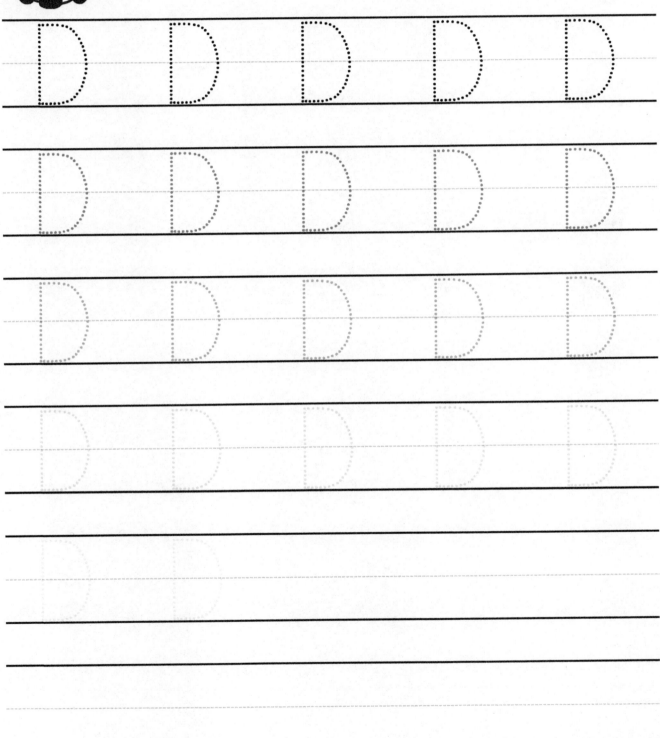

Let's be the top dog

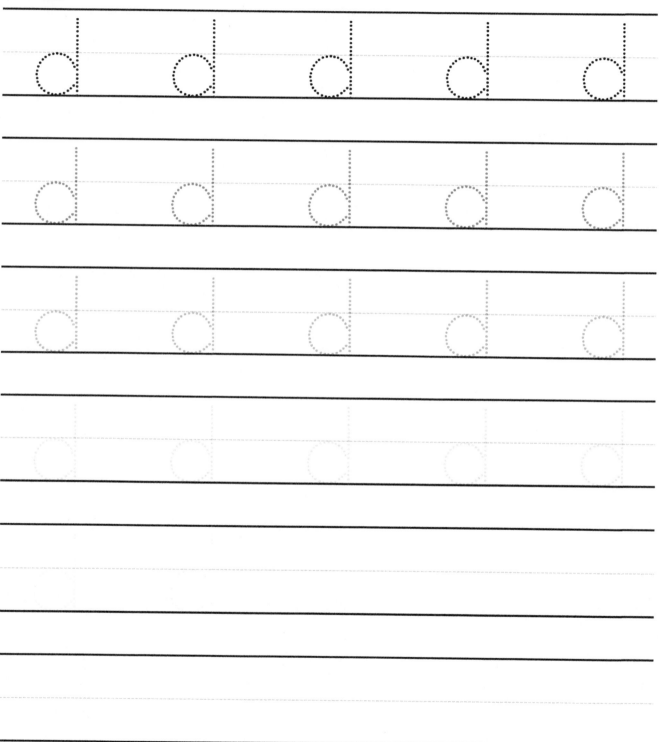

E e

E is for Elk

Trace along the alphabet character

E E E E E

E E E E E

e e e e e

e e e e e

A B C D (E) F G H I J K L M N O P Q R S T U V W X Y Z

You are doing so great!

E E E E E

E E E E E

E E E E E

a b c d (e) f g h i j k l m n o p q r s t u v w x y z

You are doing so great!

e   e   e   e   e

e   e   e   e   e

e   e   e   e   e

F f

F is for Frog

Trace along the alphabet character

F F F F F

F F F F F

f f f f f

f f f f f

The frog turned prince

The frog turned prince

Gg

G is for Goose

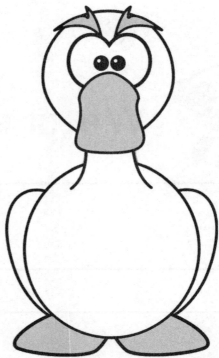

Trace along the alphabet character

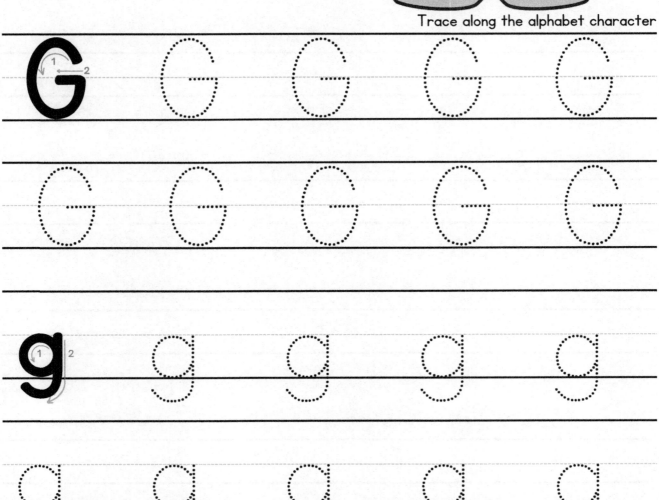

We are here. Well done!

We are here. Well done!

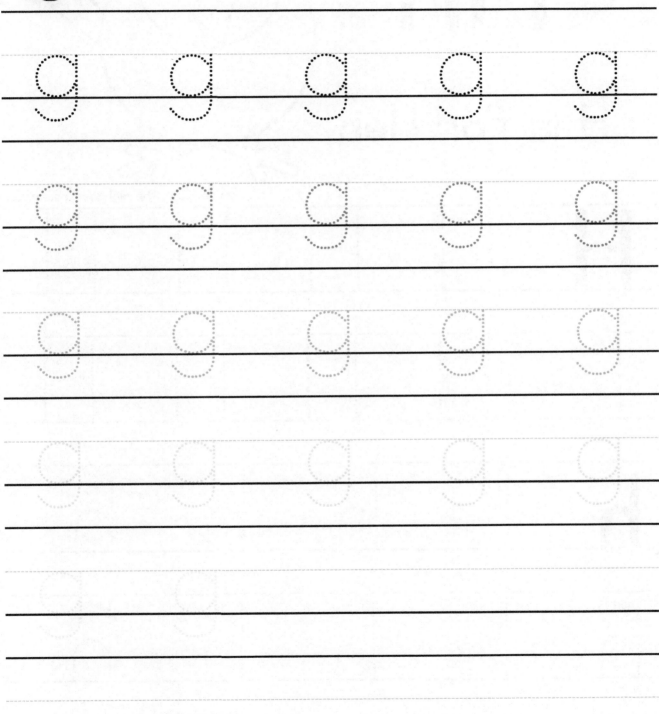

H h

H is for Hen

Trace along the alphabet character

H H H H H H

H H H H H

h h h h h

h h h h h

A B C D E F G (H) I J K L M N O P Q R S T U V W X Y Z

You are like hen's teeth

H H H H H H

H H H H H

a b c d e f g (h) i j k l m n o p q r s t u v w x y z

You are like hen's teeth

Ii

I is for Ice

2 →
1 →
3 →
I

i
2 →
1 →

You are doing so great!

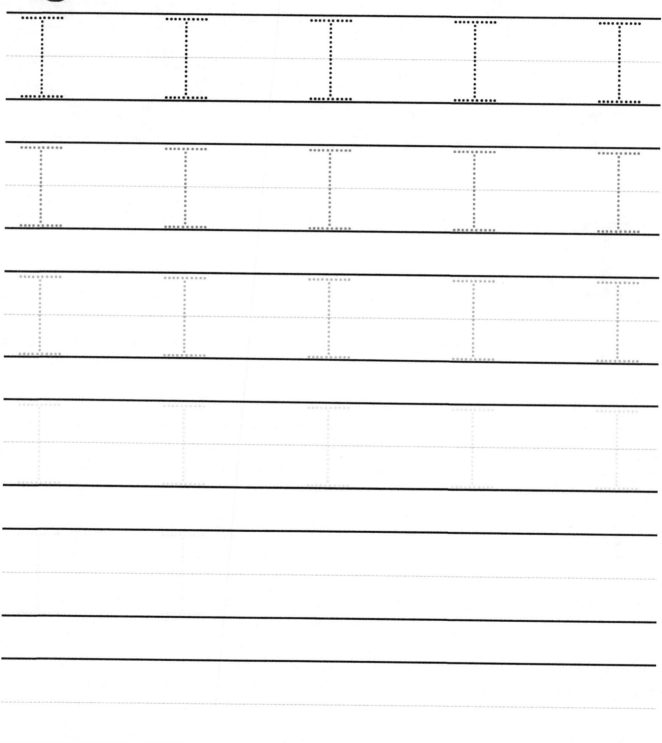

You are doing so great!

Jj

J is for Jar

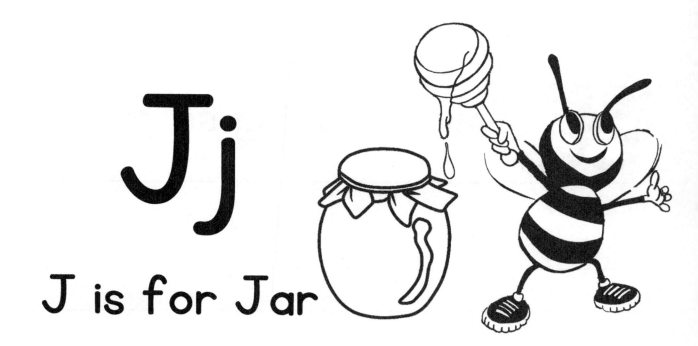

Trace along the alphabet character

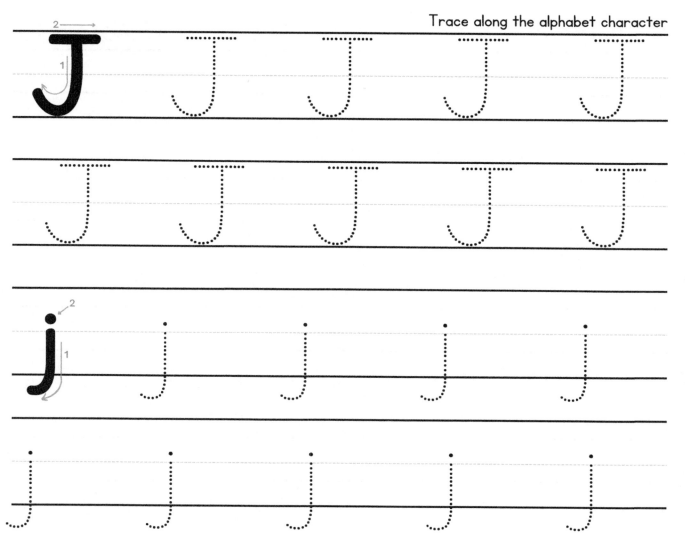

Where's the honey jar?

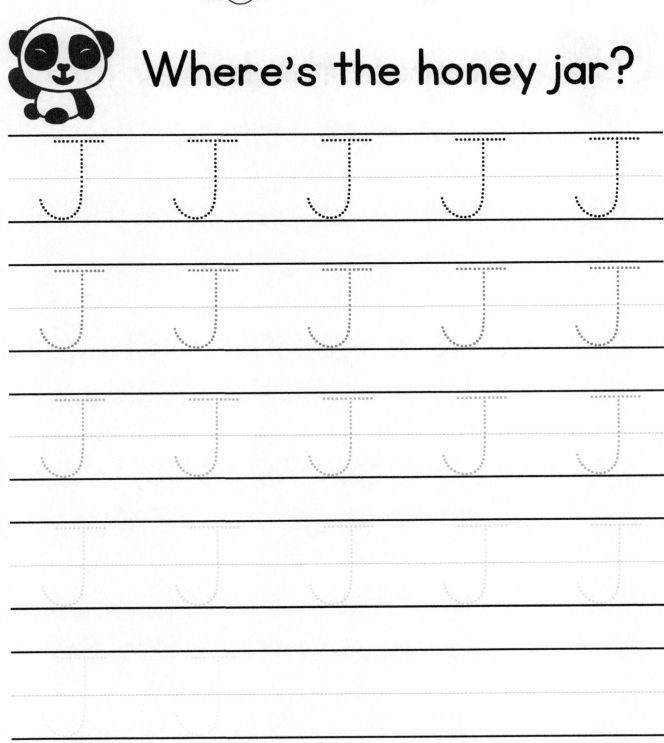

Where's the honey jar?

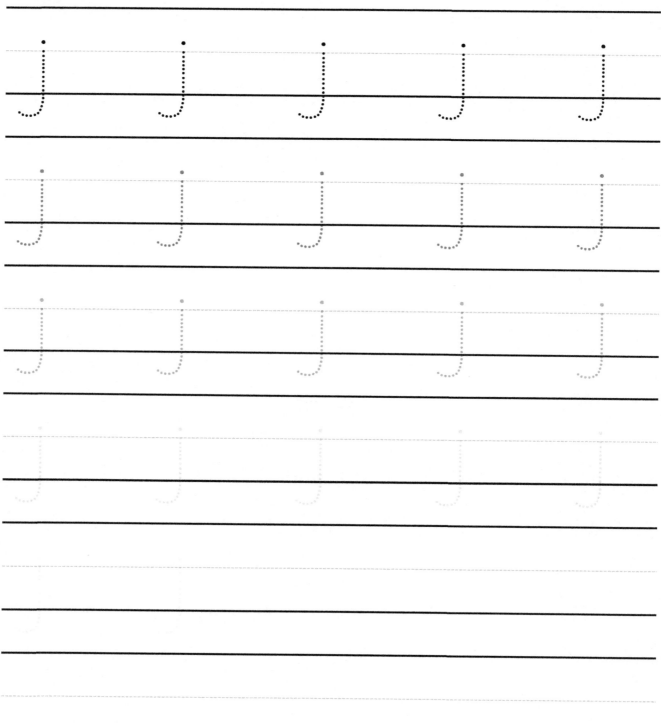

K k

K is for Koala

Trace along the alphabet character

K K K K K

K K K K K

k k k k k

k k k k k

Almost halfway...

Almost halfway...

Ll

L is for Lion

Trace along the alphabet character

L L L L L L

L L L L L L

l l l l l l

l l l l l l

A B C D E F G H I J K (L) M N O P Q R S T U V W X Y Z

Is this a lion's den?

L L L L L

Is this a lion's den?

Mm

M is for Mule

M M M M M M

M M M M M M

m m m m m m

m m m m m m

Keep it going!

Keep it going!

Nn

N is for Nut

Trace along the alphabet character

N N N N N N

N N N N N N

n n n n n

n n n n n

Tough nut to crack

Tough nut to crack

n   n   n   n   n

n   n   n   n   n

n   n   n   n   n

n   n   n   n   n

Oo

O is for Owl

Trace along the alphabet character

Wise as an owl, you!

Wise as an owl, you!

P p

P is for Pig

Trace along the alphabet character

P P P P P

P P P P P

p p p p p

p p p p p

Can't stop now!

P P P P P

P P P P P

P P P P P

P P P P P

P

Can't stop now!

p   p   p   p   p

p   p   p   p   p

p   p   p   p   p

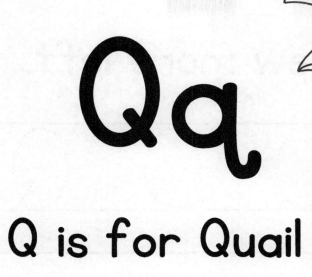 

Q is for Quail

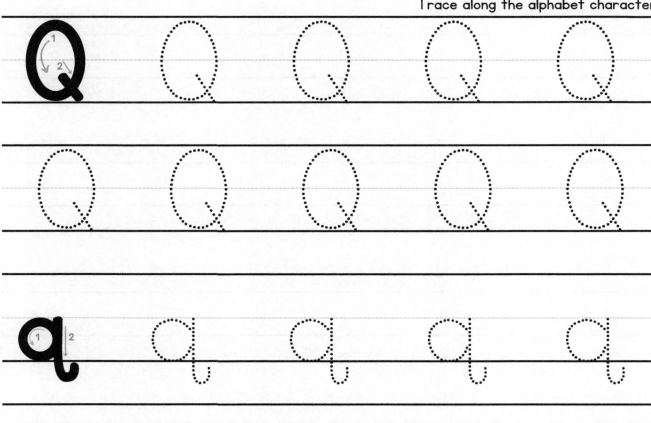

Just a few more left...

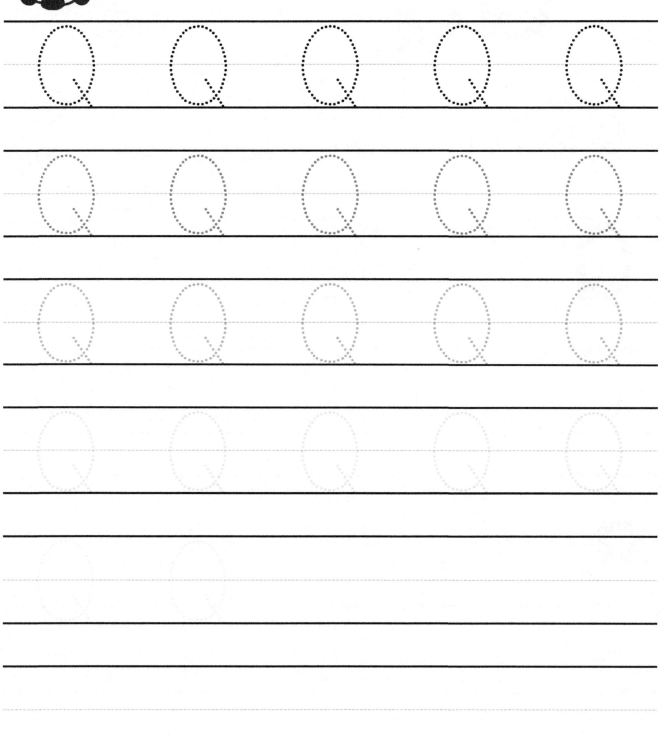

Just a few more left...

Rr

R is for Rat

Trace along the alphabet character

R R R R R R

R R R R R

r r r r r

r r r r r

A B C D E F G H I J K L M N O P Q (R) S T U V W X Y Z

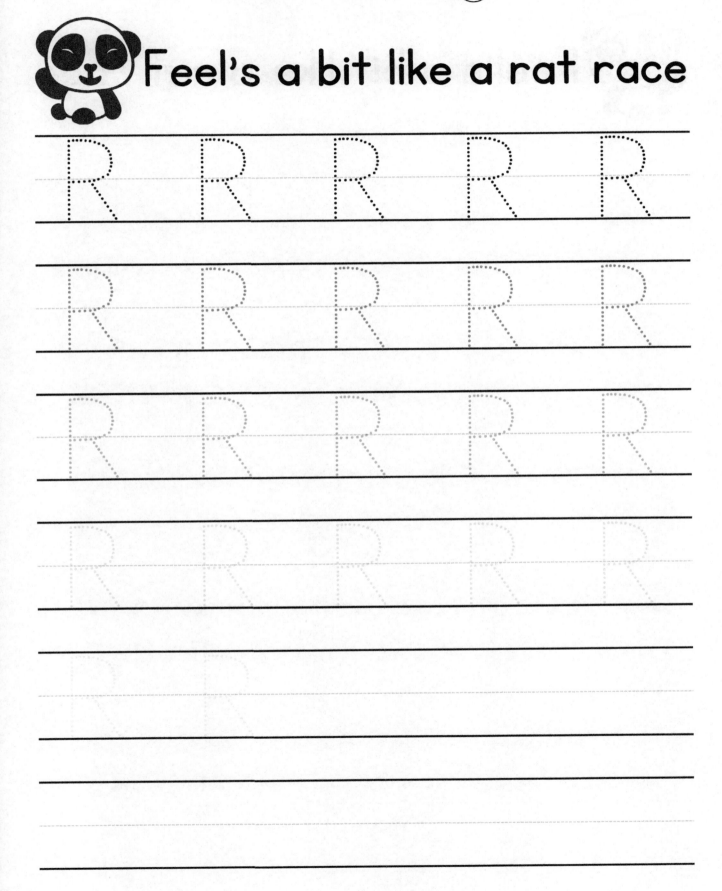

Feel's a bit like a rat race

Feel's a bit like a rat race

r r r r r

r r r r r

r r r r r

r r r r r

S s

S is for Seal

Trace along the alphabet character

S S S S S S

S S S S S S

s s s s s s

s s s s s s

Let's seal the deal

S   S   S   S   S

S   S   S   S   S

S   S   S   S   S

Let's seal the deal

T t

T is for Tiger

Trace along the alphabet character

Got the tiger by the tail

Got the tiger by the tail

Uu

U is for Udder

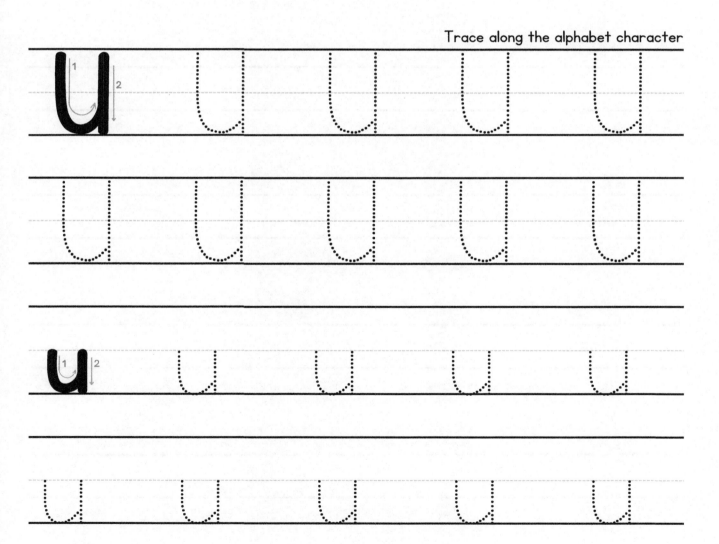

We are here. Well done!

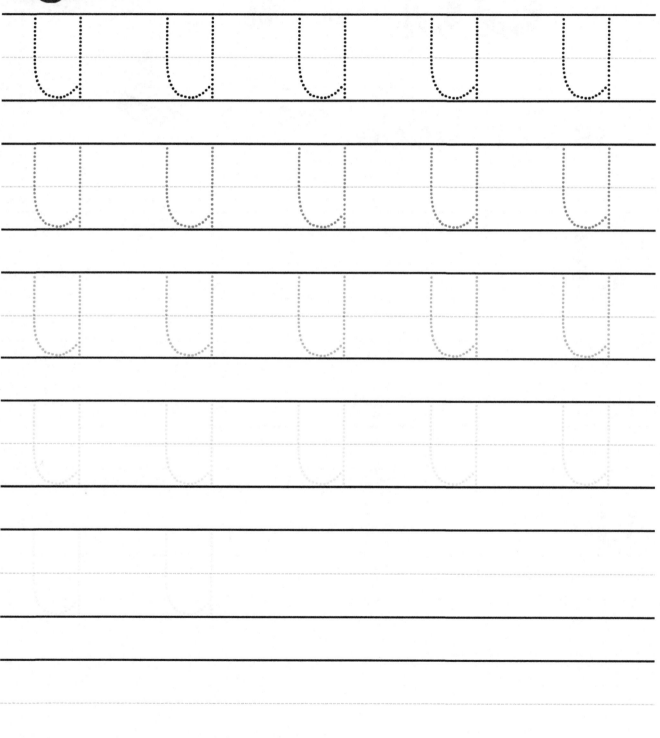

We are here. Well done!

V v

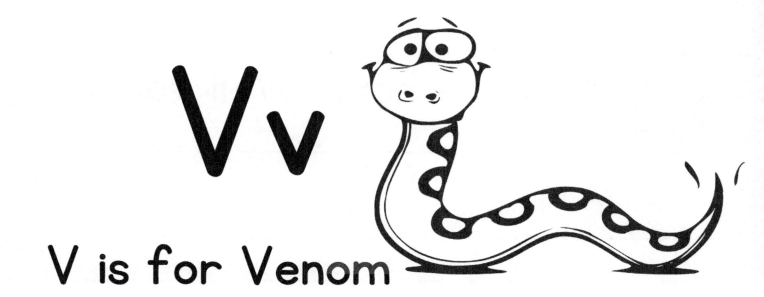

V is for Venom

Trace along the alphabet character

V V V V V V

V V V V V V

V V V V V V

V V V V V V

A B C D E F G H I J K L M N O P Q R S T U (V) W X Y Z

Vvvvery good!

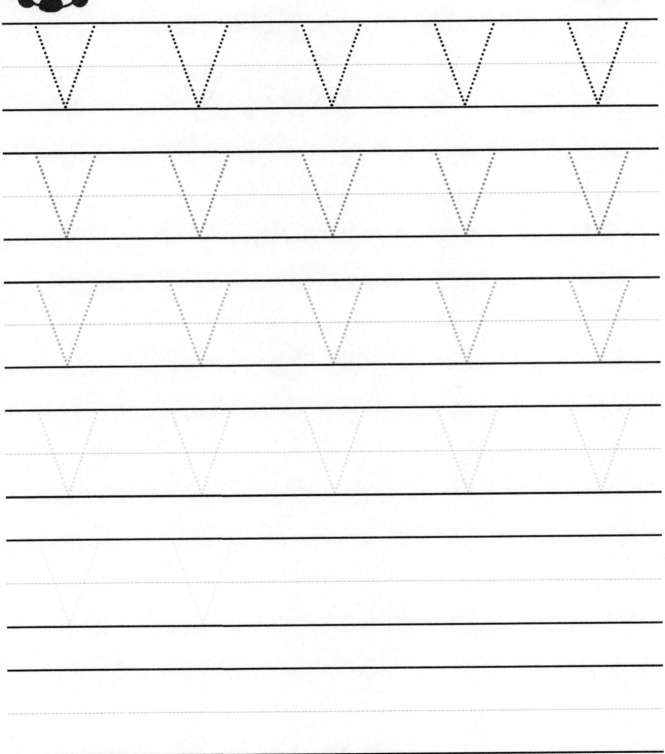

Vvvvery good!

V   V   V   V   V

V   V   V   V   V

V   V   V   V   V

V   V   V   V   V

W is for Wool

Trace along the alphabet character

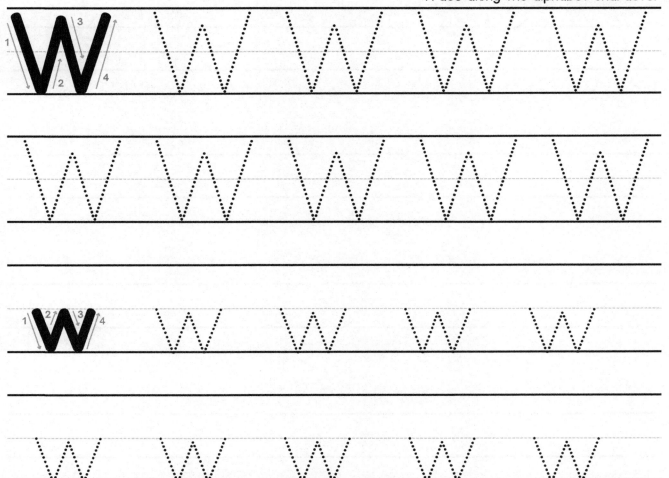

Basically there. Great!

a b c d e f g h i j k l m n o p q r s t u v w x y z

Basically there. Great!

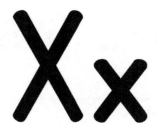

X is for X-ray

Trace along the alphabet character

Funny X, Y, Z's. Let's go!

Funny x, y, z's. Let's go!

X   X   X   X   X

X   X   X   X   X

X   X   X   X   X

Yy

Y is for Yak

Trace along the alphabet character

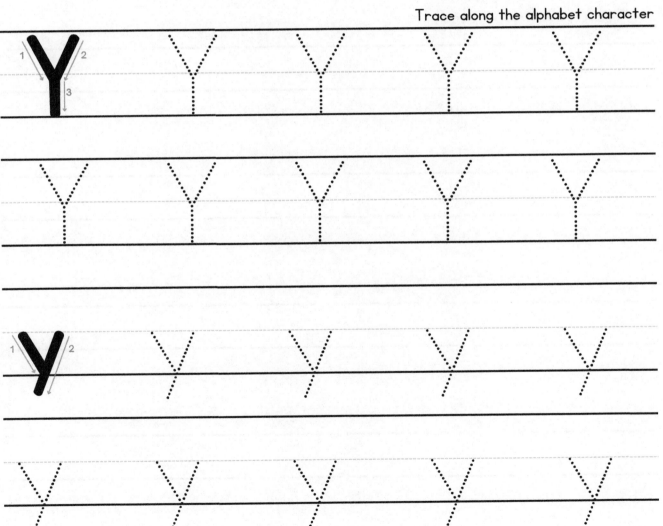

Brave the winter!

Brave the winter!

Zz

Z is for Zebra

Last one. Excellent!

Last one. Excellent!

Z   Z   Z   Z   Z

Z   Z   Z   Z   Z

Z   Z   Z   Z   Z

Part 3

Trace numbers 0 – 9

Before learning to read (or while learning to read) it is important for kids to learn holding the pencil correctly and tracing lines.

Learn how to write the numbers correctly by practicing with the following number tracing exercises.

We can color in the pictures of the number and animals associated with the number.

Hallo!

Please give me some color....

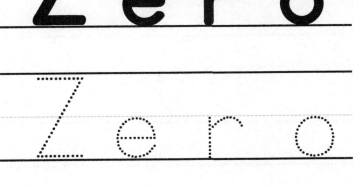

Zero

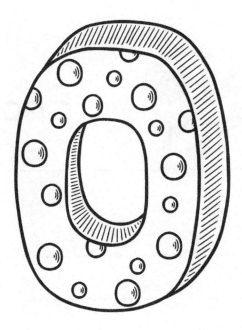

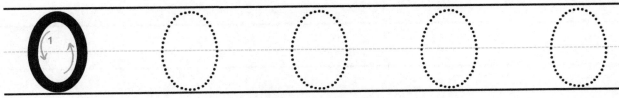

Trace along the number

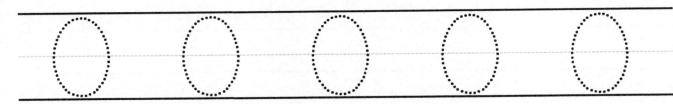

From ZERO to hero

One

One

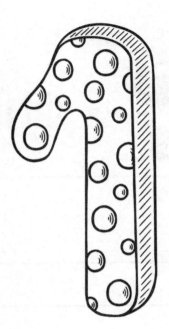

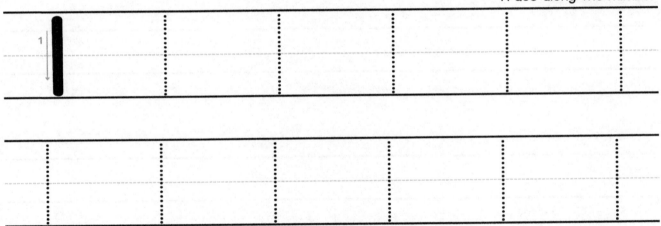

ONE of these days...

Two

Two

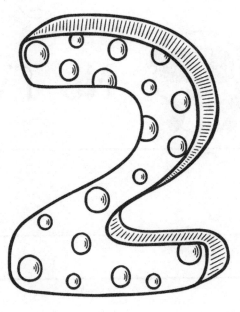

Trace along the number

2 2 2 2 2

2 2 2 2 2

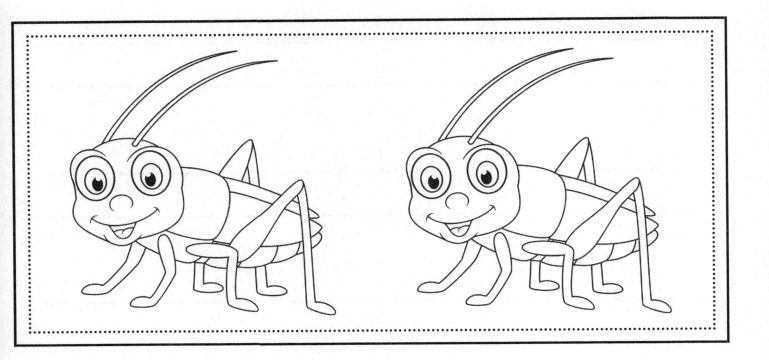

No TWO ways about it

Three

Three

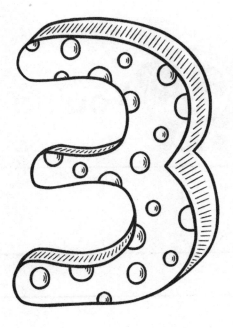

Trace along the number

3 3 3 3 3

3 3 3 3 3

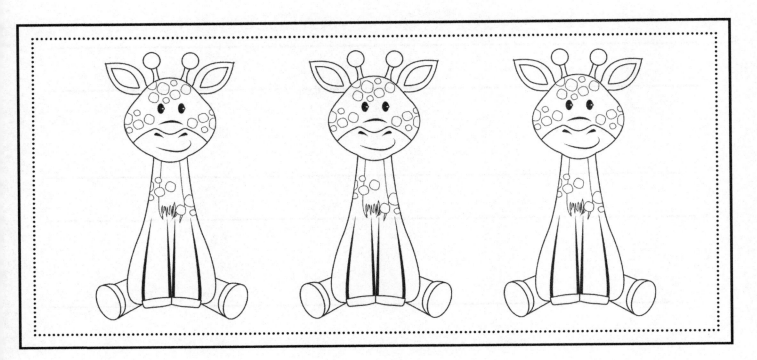

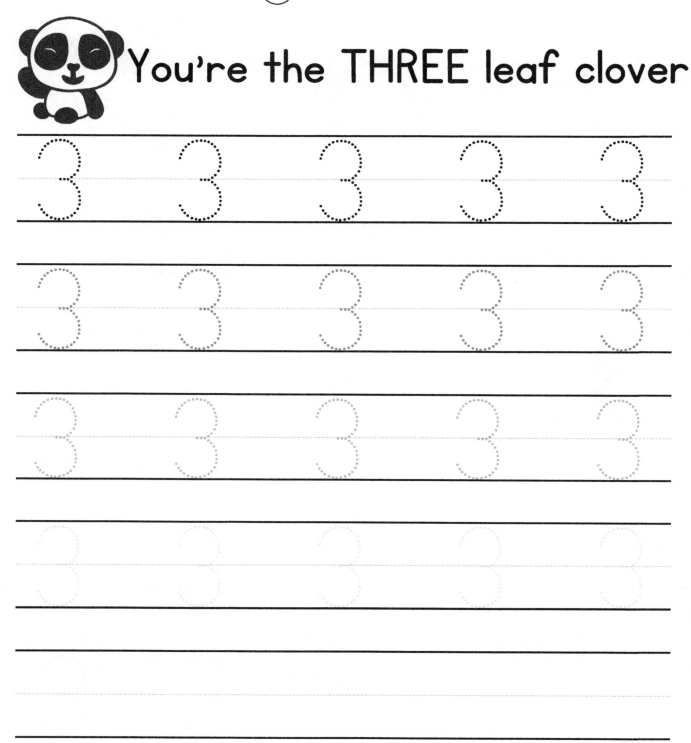

You're the THREE leaf clover

Four

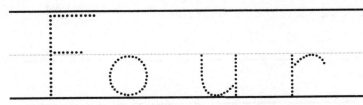

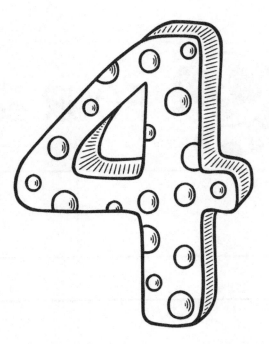

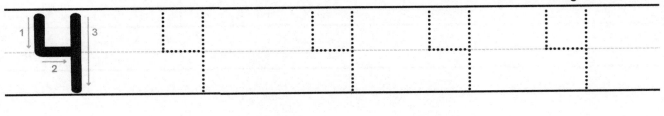

Trace along the number

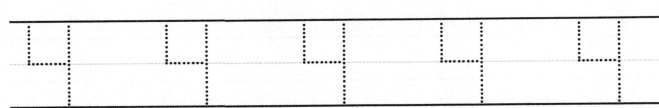

FOUR corners of the world

Five

Five

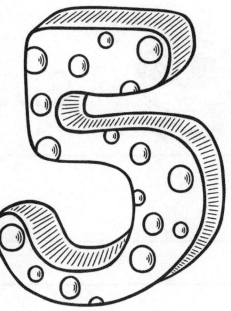

Trace along the number

5 5 5 5 5

5 5 5 5 5

Give me a high FIVE

S i x

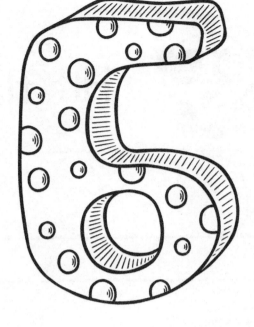

S i x

Trace along the number

6 6 6 6 6

6 6 6 6 6

Hit this one for a SIX

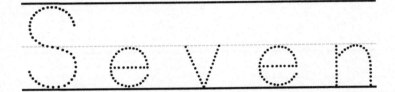 **S e v e n**

S e v e n

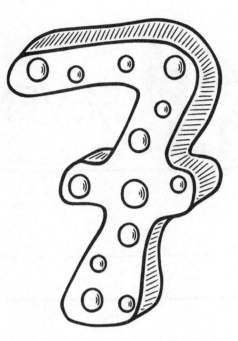

Trace along the number

7 7 7 7 7

7 7 7 7 7

SEVEN wolves are watching

7 7 7 7 7

7 7 7 7 7

7 7 7 7 7

Eight

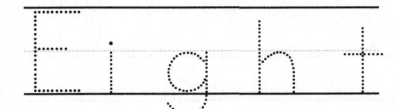

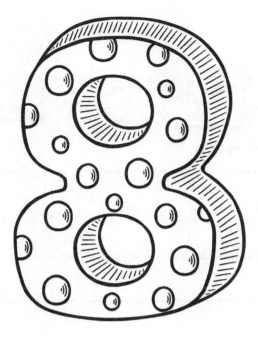

Trace along the number

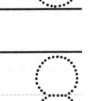

Get behind the EIGHT ball

8 8 8 8 8

8 8 8 8 8

8 8 8 8 8

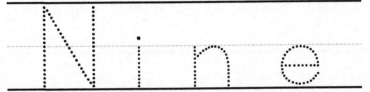

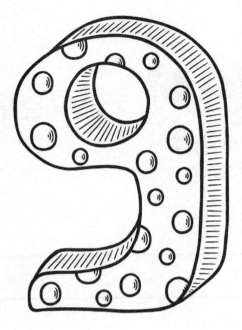

Trace along the number

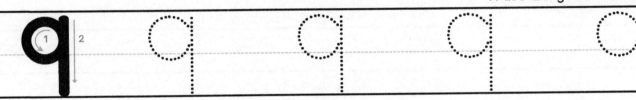

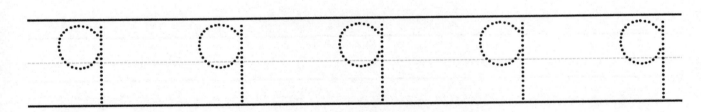

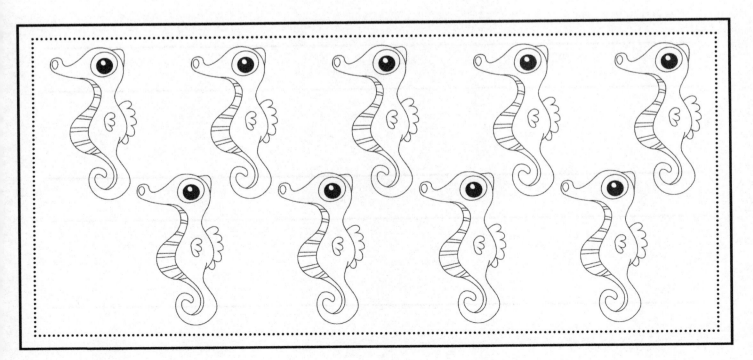

We're on cloud NINE

9 9 9 9 9

9 9 9 9 9

9 9 9 9 9

Bonus Part

Trace sight words

For a child to learn words and achieve independent practice to write words and sentences on their own, sight words are an effective technique to decode unfamiliar words.

With some guidance, copy the sight words and establish good and correct habits.

Let's test ourselves and see if we can trace sight words. We can also say them loud.

Hallo!

Please give me some color...

Sight words boost confidence.
Word recognition is the step towards learning
how to read and speak fluently.

Trace along the sight word

am   am   am

am   am   am

the   the   the

the   the   the

my   my   my

my   my   my

Once you mastered sight words, you can easily recognize half the sentence. This improves speaking, reading and comprehension.

in   in   in   in

and   and   and

of   of   of   of

Sight words promote reading comprehension. Knowledge of preschool sight words help to read and comprehend the information.

Trace along the sight word

if   if   if   if

how how how

do   do   do   do

Additionally, learning sight words help you learn to construct meaningful sentences. Once you understand text, your speech also improve.

Trace along the sight word

at at at at

our our our

so so so so

Sight words improve learning. Being familiar with sight words is an effect technique to decode unfamiliar words.

Trace along the sight word

up   up   up   up

up   up   up

can   can   can

can   can   can

go   go   go   go

go   go   go

Including sight words in your vocabulary learning sets the foundation for you to learn more complex words.

Trace along the sight word

it   it   it   it

has   has   has

no   no   no   no

Sight words are also important in helping you improve your pronunciation, writing and communication skills.

me me me me me

me me me me me

you you you you

you you you you

we we we we

we we we we

Sight words are an important tool for a foundation in learning to read. Reading only happens when you know basic words.

Trace along the sight word

to   to   to   to

to   to   to   to

are   are   are

are   are   are

at   at   at   at

at   at   at   at

Trace along the sight word

is   is   is   is

is   is   is   is

not   not   not

not   not   not

on   on   on   on

on   on   on   on

Sight words not only polish your reading skills, but also improve writing skills. Once you can read, you learn to write.

as as as as
as as as as

did did did
did did did

or or or or
or or or or

Use these few blank pages to practice some words that you will need in the future. You can find and practice your own words.

Printed in Great Britain
by Amazon

46288747R00077